Moments of Clarity

Building Hope, Finding Comfort

Dion Thorpe

MISSION POSSIBLE PRESS

Inspirational Development Series

Creating Legacies through Absolute Good Works

AbsoluteGood.com
MomentsofClarityBook.com

The Mission is Possible.
Sharing love and wisdom for the young and "young
at heart,"
Expanding minds,
Restoring kindness through
Good thoughts, feelings, and attitudes
is our intent.
May you thrive and be good in all you are and all
you do…
Be Cause U.R. Absolute Good!

Dedication

To God first and foremost, who is the head of my life and who made it possible for me to put this in thought.

To my mother Anna "Lil' Bit" Thorpe for giving me life, love and morals.

Acknowledgements

To all the praying grandmothers, the motivating fathers, the encouraging mothers, the heckling aunts and uncles, the supportive siblings, nosey neighbors and to all of my brothers and sisters in Christ.

To Robert Holt, thank you for encouraging me to seek the will of God, making it comfortable for me to see that there is a power greater than me at work and for holding my hand during my travels in darkness.

Special thanks to Michael Lawrence, Roderick B., Christel R., Marnique M., Glenda A., Gaylord R. and countless other friends.

To my wife Yolanda, thank you for listening to the meditations and for letting me know that they were okay. Thanks for allowing me to move forward in this process and for being with me in my weakest hours. I love you very much.

"…Take courage and be a man. Observe the requirements of the Lord your God, and follow all his ways. Keep the decrees, commands, regulations, and laws written in the Law of Moses so that you will be successful in all you do and wherever you go."

1Kings 2:2-3
New Living Translation (NLT)
Holy Bible

New Beginnings

I am willing to share my discoveries and experiences with others because I know that life takes connection and relationships.

The bonds that we build and the unity that we establish supports our lives, our communities and the structure needed to excel in today's society.

Members of our families often do the best they can. Whether they faltered, failed or not, their actions affected us.

Most of us have baggage from the past and it is sometimes difficult to live up to the status of role model without having had some of our own.

I ask God to give you and me the wisdom, courage and presence to be who He would have us to be.

~ Dion

To Understand Where These Meditations are Leading You...

We eventually redefine our beliefs and understanding to the point where we see that our greatest need is for knowledge of God's Will for us and that He is the strength to carry that out.

January—I identify with the elements of selfishness, the past and mistakes, which helps me to connect and begin to move forward. I must know what I am facing and that I have purpose. Often we try to take on what society is putting on us. But we have to take on what God is putting on us.

February—Helps me seek that source of strength.

March—Allows me to understand that there is a Power greater than myself, I am relating and finding comfort.

April—Now that I am moving forward, what am I going to do?

May, June and July—I've got to continue to seek that Power greater than myself; I stay in tune with these teachings as seasons change. As life happens, the way I see myself, handle myself and treat others grows – as with my faith.

August, September and October—I choose to put what I've learned into play through my relationships with those in society.

November—Where am I now? How has the studying, learning and understanding allowed me to enjoy this freedom?

December—I'm just truly grateful.

January 1—Call to Action

Going to those extremes—we've got to stop to see things clearly.

How many times have you told your children, job or a loved one you were going to be there? Or yourself that this would be the last time? Or told someone, that no matter what, you were not going to be a "no call no show"?

We did so much lying that we began to believe the lies ourselves. One of the first things I had to learn to do was STOP. Stopping gave me that moment of clarity to think if I wanted to live or die.

When we don't think it's possible, we are placed in a position that forces us to stop because of circumstances that we have created.

Now it's time to walk the walk, then to talk the talk. For it's better to move your hips instead of your lips.

January 2

Happiness is a blessing we receive from our Higher Power when we carry a clear message of hope.

For the first time in many years we feel excited about this newfound change we have begun to accept, however we fall short of acceptance due to the lifestyle we have lived.

January 3

Happiness is a blessing that we receive from our Higher Power, perhaps something that we haven't experienced in some time. It's that very moment of being happy that keeps us excited, and realizing that change starts with admitting.

As we gain the courage to surrender, we start to be free from the bondage of self. The pressure relief valve that we've been looking for allows us to be honest and open with ourselves.

January 4

My structure was built on self-will and self-indulgence. This kept me confined in my selfish deeds.

Often on this journey of life we find ourselves wandering off into that playground of thoughts – the very ones that influence us to act out.

It's no wonder that we were born with an abundance of natural desires that we sometimes lose on our way because we let them take over and exceed their purpose. It's not strange that we let these thoughts go wild and then that desire becomes what is normal for us.

Hope is born, new understanding is gained and we no longer allow our selfishness to drive us blindly. The beauty of service is in knowing that God's will for me will sink deeper into my soul the more I become obedient to His will and not mine own.

January 5

Identifying the fear underneath the defect gives us recognition to see that it's a feeling we have to face and that we don't want to lose.

In facing the feeling there is value because letting go of the fear is the whole purpose of learning, working and believing in the process.

January 6

When situations arise which destroy my serenity, I don't have to stay in my emotions and become overly sensitive about them.

I've learned that when I change my attitude I face my situation – with better understanding.

January 7

I was influenced by other people's expectations and that controlled my thoughts, feelings and brought about more pain.

The more I began to understand that these are liabilities and defects that have manifested into my life, the easier things became. They are just symptoms of my problems.

Going outside of self brings new vision, hope and grace, and then no matter what, I can bear it through the dark and negative side of my defects to arise on a brighter side.

January 8

I'm learning today about how to stay out of self and move into self-awareness.

Somewhere along the way many of my feelings and destructive actions have developed through my life experiences. I have since learned to recognize what is happening.

I now know that most of my dilemmas, and what I was feeling, was what I was supposed to feel at that moment. However, I was just frightened.

Through a personal relationship with God and a program of action, I understand that I don't have to act out on feelings anymore.

January 9

Being held hostage by our self-centeredness, we are confined to a four-block radius, robbing ourselves of the benefits that God has to offer.

Living from one corner to the next, trapped by obsession and compulsion, we get up off that corner when we seek to live in obedience to the will of God.

January 10

Realizing how our emotions victimized us, we come to open our minds and eyes to the new possibilities found in our new direction from a personal relationship built on faith and within the protection of God's grace.

January 11

Blaming and prejudices must be recognized.

We admit our shortcomings that have caused us to keep a closed mind.

Acceptance and admittance begin my procession to freedom.

January 12

Being trapped in bondage, feeding off of selfishness kept us sick.

As we accept this as being dis-ease, it is a relief that we are building our new foundation and awareness.

January 13

There are many situations in life where we can insist on having our will and way, but that doesn't usually work.

We meditate for the courage to change when these moments surface – reaching out of the gutter of hurt, pain and bad choices.

January 14

I had gotten to the point where I was unable to make effective choices in any part of my life and my life became unmanageable.

I am surrendering and I am willing to make changes.

January 15

No longer do I isolate myself from the rest of the world.

Today I'm living in a program of action and I learn more each day about how to deflate my ego.

January 16

Now that I'm beginning to work on the structure of my foundation, I still question myself. Facing my fears is allowing me to grow past my defects.

January 17

I release the past and all excess baggage. I try harmonizing and restoring situations.

I give back to the world around me rather than just taking.

January 18

It's *all right* to admit defeat to the dis-ease.

We must endure and get through the rough spots because taking things too seriously can cause us to get stuck and stay stubborn. We can find the humor in difficult situations even when it's dark and lonely.

Finding humor in difficult situations helps us to develop our gifts.

January 19

Along this journey of hope and in our quest to find comfort, we pick up experiences and tools along the way to help us build.

Change is not immediate yet; I focus on working through my problems with courage and honesty as I pray for faith to become the very foundation on which I stand.

January 20

God's will may seem to be uncomfortable to reach for when your mind is troubled.

When you are willing to listen to it, you may feel strange. As you work through that feeling, and start praying, you may find yourself telling the truth, opening up, and taking the suggestions. This allows you to carry a clear message of hope to those around you as well.

January 21

We rob ourselves of energy when we question the road before us and remain disconnected.

We must search out and be ready for the currents of new life and hope.

January 22

Many of my defects become more objectionable as I tap into a power greater than myself.

That's when I move from denial to honesty and acceptance.

January 23

I am willing to stop trying to force things to make them happen.

God gives me courage to live life honestly.

Today I build, not destroy.

January 24

With a positive, helpful attitude, and learning how to relax, we have new experiences and gain knowledge and wisdom. We find that the more our thoughts are awakened to the greater good in society, our hearts open up as well.

January 25

When you practice meditating from the inside, it leads to infinite light and peace. This is a process that takes time and focus. As you become more comfortable mediating you may start to realize that fear had been a roadblock.

Fear of change is groundless even though it doesn't feel that way. As you continue to mediate, that source of pain is removed from your life and peace replaces it.

January 26

Life lessons and experiences are important.

Learning from our mistakes will help us stay grounded. With the right input, new thoughts will help us start to fly. We then find our lives enriched with spiritual awakening.

January 27

Noticing where we are helps us to know what hasn't been working. Guilt sometimes stops us from moving forward.

An excellent way to begin clearing and releasing guilt is to drop back into reality.

We slow down and work on spiritual principles because we want to grow.

January 28

I am ready to face each day with hope. When things are damaging or hurtful to me, I drop my judgmental mind and seek out understanding from a power greater.

January 29

Each stage of life is unfolding; all fears and excuses are stones. When we find willingness to believe, our lost dreams will come true.

January 30

The beauty I find on this journey lies in knowing that my life with God as my center gives me something real to live for.

Life with Him improves everything and brings me to the lessons and joy that I need.

January 31

You are growing and gaining serenity every day.

Relief comes in the form of patience and tolerance found in admitting the truth about your lifestyle, rather than hiding or denying it.

February 1

God has seen fit to give us the blessing of life. We then go out to get experience filled with many lessons.

Now that the stage is set, we must take our respective places and enjoy the gift He has given. We begin to trudge this road with courage and honesty into to a state of happiness.

February 2

Notice how we react when certain feelings come up. We get trapped in thought about what decisions to make in that moment.

When we step outside ourselves we are able to see God working.

February 3

Understanding the havoc I created and trying to repair the destruction, I am open to the energy that flows around me.

I recognize the many miracles in my life.

February 4

We get so busy living that we forget to have a life.

Openly, we admit the nature of our struggles and realize that it's principles before personalities that will pull us through.

February 5

Gradually with patience, humility and a lot of gratitude, we will tap into a true Power. We learn that change is how we move forward in our lives.

February 6

Harmonizing can achieve so much more than yelling and fighting.

With the willingness to change ourselves, open-mindedness can unlock doors to the spiritual awakening for which we have prayed.

February 7

The principles we learn become a mainstay of life today, if you are going to spread anything, let it be joy and goodwill.

February 8

After putting together my blueprint for construction, the cement used is mixed together with surrender and admittance, and then I smooth it with a willingness that makes it solid.

February 9

Now we begin to walk the path that is to become the journey. We trudge this road for happiness. The reward is peace of mind.

February 10

At one time life was a constant battle. I was trying to figure it out on my own and it kept hurting. The pain outweighed the pleasure.

I realize those wounds need to be healed and it has to come from inside.

I am discovering how to change my attitudes and I am letting go of the defects in order to heal.

February 11

I used to be a victim of my expectations, choices and dishonesty.

Often I fought against living life on life's terms, not taking responsibility, not doing the right things for the right reasons, nor standing up and making mature choices, which created uncontrollable situations.

Today I am using spiritual principles to let go and strengthen me.

February 12

As I become more spiritual I observe a rippling effect. I learn to relax in the safety of God's will and guidance.

When I need clarity I stay alert for the opportunity to practice principles that continue to move me forward.

February 13

I must sacrifice some of my personality traits, as false pride can be inflated through prestige.

As I study my lifestyle and my priorities change, I don't let my cozy nest become a locked and confining box.

February 14

I realize that my life is in the hands of a Master Craftsman. He is allowing me to experience and recognize how good it feels to be me.

February 15

As we come to know and understand God, we must continue to study and to learn His will for us.

As I grow, I share and provide help and service to others.

February 16

We grow through life not knowing the morals, values and the best of what society has to offer.

Misinformation keeps me locked into things that don't always work for me.

Through experience and understanding we gather up knowledge and wisdom to know that there is a difference.

With courage and anticipation each day gets brighter.

February 17

I am to be bold enough to ask for guidance.

I don't let emotions define my reality. I take a few moments to listen for answers in meditation.

February 18

The part we play on this journey is that we must do the legwork. Now that we've got the material gathered, we are continuing to build.

February 19

We can't allow shame and guilt to be reasons to stop building. We are continuously learning from our mistakes.

This growth is helping put our past behind us and is preparing us for our future.

February 20

Conflicts put us into situations that we used to run from. Eventually, we come to learn what to repair and fix. Deep down inside each and every one of us is that place that helps us to see miracles.

We seek God to stop running.

February 21

The resources that I relied on were not sufficient and they failed me utterly. Now I am becoming honest, open-minded, responsible and forgiving.

February 22

Guidance from God is turning my worst faults into my greatest assets.

When we seek to restore balance, our hearts and our souls will heal.

February 23

Through awareness of our Higher Power we are coming to find peace through prayer and meditation.

We are improving our contact with God as we clean our closets.

February 24

In working in our closet we come to ask God to remove what's blocking the light. Once exposed, we see that we have a bunch of garbage we've collected.

February 25

When we don't acknowledge the magnitude of the miracle that we have received, how can we take pride in our accomplishments?

This is why we clean out the trash – so we can see the miracles.

February 26

I'm learning to see how my defects have allowed me to live in darkness. I understand that separating what I feel from what I do brings clarity to my character.

February 27

Pain is something that most of us have in common, though our situations and experiences may be different. When we struggle to correct our problems alone, they usually continue.

Remedies and solutions come through conscious contact with Him.

February 28

Giving up – admitting and surrendering to a dependence on God – is the force needed to drive my spirituality.

Opening that old closet and cleaning it out allows me to be in the passenger seat and enjoy the ride.

I am comfortable with self enough to share with someone the true nature of me.

I ask for God's unchanging hand to hold as I walk through this storm.

Leap Year Bonus – February 29

Before I open my mouth, I ask myself a simple question...

Could it be a tinge of guilt or fear that has caused me to not want to be fearless, courageous and confident to say and feel the right things?

March 1

Sometimes, I don't like what I feel. Being humble means being open, teachable, willing and courageous.

I accept courage to face what I don't want to feel. With humility as my guide, I experience freedom and relief.

Though I sometimes feel doubt, I am trusting in God to feel better.

March 2

In order for me to move freely, I have to stop denying myself opportunities and possibilities.

I recognize that I've taken on some emotions that don't work for me. I start to clear them out and begin to expect miracles.

March 3

When we don't protect ourselves we soak up other people's feelings.

When this happens, we do a great deal of injustice to our process and future.

We have to ask God daily to remove our shortcomings, rinse us off, and bind us in His armor.

March 4

We must learn how to walk in the darkness to find peace, a peace that can only be enjoyed from the inside out.

March 5

When I consider others, it decreases my selfishness and increases self-awareness and my ability to be of service to people. I increase positive thoughts and activities as I share hope and courage.

March 6

Our foundation is becoming more solid. We find freedom in our hearts and minds when we walk into the light. Our daily walk is becoming brighter and more stable.

March 7

We can enjoy the benefits of life by being normal, although that alone is not enough. The importance of prayer is to use it as the key to unlock the door to new realities.

March 8

Humility will bring balance into our life, for we now know how vulnerable we are. Freedom is not found by being in the company of others but in the working of a spiritual program.

March 9

Often I focus on my problems and frustrations. When I think of the things I have gone through and the bad decisions I have made, it's too easy to get caught up and that causes more problems.

I must let them go in order to press forward, understanding that life as I have come know it will never be the same.

At this moment I am working to exercise my faith.

March 10

We are crippled because we are not humble. When we begin to understand our relationship with God we are able to feel our spiritual nature.

This helps me to have confidence and create realistic expectations based on faith in Him rather than pride in me.

March 11

Let go of judgment and resentment as this can cause more grief. Going back and reliving what happened in the past doesn't help in the heat of the moment or during the middle of your pain.

Something is missing.

When we recognize the harm we have done, we then eliminate the pride that blocks the blessings.

March 12

When God picked me up, I was emotionally, physically and spiritually defeated. By dusting myself off, I step up to the plate. By accepting life with Him, I gain serenity.

March 13

We can't always be sure that things will work out, but if we examine the parts that are troubling us then maybe we will discover that it is the experience, not the outcome, that is the true prize.

March 14

How many times have I allowed resentment and foolish expectations to destroy my morals and find myself beaten again?

Spiritual principles offer me the freedom to distinguish between what I can and can't do.

March 15

We're enriched by our experiences and we know the difference between what to work on and what we must turn over.

Being grateful for whatever we have always turns what we have into more.

I become willing to know, want, and desire God's will for me.

March 16

Today life is beginning to move forward; our willingness to participate in the solution has increased.

We no longer focus on just the big problems. We also recognize the small ones.

March 17

Are we discovering more of ourselves and who we really are?

Are we actually facing and working through our problems?

Are we learning to imitate the love that God has for us?

Or, are we still making all the decisions?

March 18

For so long all I did was be dishonest. This made my unrealistic life full of difficult times. I often wondered if things were going to get better.

Honesty is one of the fundamental principles of my spiritual process.

March 19

Every time we stop working on being honest our plans fail. I realize it will be that way as I am still working toward being humble and remembering to be grateful.

March 20

"I have moved past the point in my life where my drug use is not a secret. Exposing it was very much needed in order for me to grow." ~ Dion

My Higher Power has always been with me, even when I didn't know it. And faith has allowed me to develop willingness.

March 21

I'm cutting back on the "weeds" of deceit, cheating, and dishonesty.

I'm learning something new that gives me courage to push against the many challenges.

I find relief from those things that used to cause me shame.

March 22

I'm grateful for the liabilities that have been my defects. It's my assets with which I'm learning to fly right.

The same principle applies to whatever secrets that may be a burden.

March 23

Today I take suggestions from others who choose to live by spiritual principles; their lifestyles have been examples in restoring and shaping my thoughts.

March 24

We must truly seek for ourselves this newfound freedom that comes from change.

We learn to use our frustration to motivate us to surrender, believe and understand that change is transformation.

March 25

I find that I trust myself to do what is necessary when I stop fighting with the problems.

Natural conditioning is about taking steps that help me to think, cope and make it through every single day. This allows me to live in the solutions.

March 26

Our obsession with being selfish has selfishly molded our actions. Things like lying, manipulation and cheating don't work.

I recognize that these defects work against me.

March 27

We find in our developing relationship with God that instead of depleting our energy fighting, we let go. Selfishness is no longer shaping our thoughts.

March 28

The more I study and build my spiritual structure, I begin to feel it's not just about changing.

It is helping me to develop a stronger character.

March 29

Humility keeps me open to change. I keep myself available to be of service and to do God's will. In God I find the surest source of satisfaction.

March 30

How are we to fight what's ungodly, and what is seemingly unbeatable and invincible?

It is through faith in a Power greater than myself and the continual practice of spiritual principles in which I develop that needed assurance.

March 31

We are learning to change what we say and how we speak so that we don't shoot down the possibilities and blessings that God has for us.

April 1

Today I stop and ask myself: "Is that 'first thought' something to act on or learn from?"

If I move past that instant and take a deeper look, I appreciate that this has happened to teach me something new.

I experience a sure sense of direction and emotional security as I make thoughtful decisions and strategic steps.

April 2

My heart is softening up and true peace from within is becoming more of a reality for me. I have serenity with self and others. God is the freedom and Light is the understanding that shines through our differences.

April 3

It is easy to stay grateful and humble when everything runs smoothly.

When people and situations happen that compromise our peace, that's when we start to question.

We're not always right in what we believe or how we react.

I thank God for showing me His design for living, especially when I want to act up.

April 4

Stay open to examining and changing your beliefs and ideals.

It's this continual awareness of God who loves you unconditionally through the learning, teaching, growing and the new decisions you make which strengthens you.

April 5

Sometimes we get what we ask for and that can bring trouble. If I'm honest enough with myself I can cleanse my mind of these unhealthy thoughts.

Wisdom is something that has to be worked toward especially when it's least expected.

I thank God that things don't often happen according to my little plan.

April 6

We are preparing ourselves to overcome our defects, to face our fears and to completely transform our lives as we stay connected to God.

That same God who was there during my active addictions, bad decisions, shameful moments, biggest failures and unhealthy thoughts, is the same God that supplies my glorious freedom.

April 7

We can't continue being caught up in the foolish philosophies of others. As I learn to study for myself, I am nurtured.

I grow in wisdom and understanding.

April 8

Sometimes I'm living in darkness. I have unhealthy thoughts or simply don't know, like or understand what or why certain things are happening.

In order to be what God wants me to be I first must recognize that seeking Him brings light.

I willingly receive knowledge and understanding from my Higher Power.

April 9

We can't straddle the fence when it comes to seeking God's will.

We either get off the fence and work, or sit there waiting for something to happen.

April 10

When I begin to worry about the struggles of life, the possible wrong decisions I have made and could have made, that's me taking my will back.

How can I say that I have a belief in God's will if I am trying to handle everything on my own?

Calling on my Higher Power gives me strength, lifts my burdens and rescues me. Knowing this keeps me grateful.

April 11

An awaking of the spirit is one of the most valuable gifts that we can receive. Don't spend all of your time second- and third-guessing yourself.

In each day there is a purpose for you being.

April 12

The more we continue to examine our lives we start to see the importance of forgiveness.

If I'm not willing to forgive then that freedom and peace I long for will only remain a desire.

April 13

Our new way of life is more than just hope and desire. In the past, most of the time we had been running in place.

Instead of staying stagnant, I encourage, teach and motivate outside of self to be of service.

I am becoming a vehicle to carry a clear message to others as well.

April 14

What was once a personal adventure has now become a quest for God's unchanging hand.

I'm now learning to maintain this freedom and increase my dependence on God.

April 15

I am more equipped to check myself with God leading the way. I stop, drop and listen.

I have more strength and courage to do His will and not my own.

April 16

During my time in darkness I lived with a lot of self-inflicted defects.

Today I'm not playing catch up; I'm just learning to cleanse my character through a spiritual program.

April 17

Jealousy of the success or happiness of others brings about resentment.

This form of fear prevents us from developing any kind of reliance on a Higher Power.

Today I celebrate who I am and where I am no matter what.

April 18

For years I allowed resentments to eat away at the core of my spirit, today I'm able to open up to be honest, open-minded and willing.

April 19

Now that I'm learning to understand God, an explosion of reds, blacks, and yellows pour out, for I'm able to see my true self.

Tears of joy and relief are the blessings that come when I do the right thing.

April 20

Just because we are in a process of change doesn't give us our humanity pass.

Those whom we have harmed the most are still watching us closely.

April 21

I understand what I have done in my past. If I continue to let it stand between me and my desire to move toward serenity, I will stumble.

I've asked for the courage to face my fears and I accept that through God's grace, I receive it.

April 22

How often would we like to put the past behind us and just live in "the golden day of time," you know, the American dream of apple pie and ice cream?

The good news?

My story hasn't ended yet and I'm moving toward understanding.

I know that it's not what happens in life, it's how I choose to react, accept and respond that really matters as I enjoy what God is providing for me.

April 23

No longer do I feel that God owes me anything.

I no longer try to convince myself that people have to live up to my expectations.

The more I serve the more rewards I'll receive.

April 24

I had to look at the damage I had done, doing vicious things and allowing animalistic tendencies to take over and dominate me, which caused pain and confusion.

When it got to be too much, I started getting in touch with the human experience, along with the emotions of sorrow and joy.

When I have truly had enough, I seek and stay in God's will so that I allow His spirit to flow and me to let go.

April 25

We recognize and deal with what the presence of guilt and pride produces in our lives.

We do an inventory so that we can look at each experience, each decade and each chapter in our book of life.

With that information we better prepare ourselves for moments of clarity and better living.

April 26

With the help of my Higher Power, I develop virtues of brotherly love, relief and truth. I seek ways to help myself and others overcome selfishness, dis-eases and challenges.

April 27

We cannot change difficult people in our lives.

Instead of being sucked in and reacting to what's happening in the moment, I work to develop the courage to stop and think about what's most important.

I recognize where I was wrong and honestly seek a better attitude and positive outcomes.

I admit that it's my actions that I need to change.

April 28

I have to believe that I am who I am and where I am at this moment is for a reason.

I stop allowing my self-imposed limitations to prevent me from realizing my potential.

April 29

As I face the reality of the harm I had done, I remember that there is a difference between knowing about the power of gratitude and actually applying gratitude in my life.

April 30

What's important in my relationship with God is that I stand before Him knowing that I don't have to be the lifelong victim of my experience.

I am thankful for my life as it is right now.

May 1

Now that I've stopped living in darkness, lying in fear and acting out selfishly, I can move about freely as my steps to self-improvement have small beginnings.

It starts out when I share openly in the light, not being afraid to ask for help, take a few simple suggestions and honestly face my problems. This is before I can truly begin doing for others outside of self.

Courage develops from the change of my attitude, emotions, and behavior so that I can feel comfortable walking on this journey.

May 2

Before I had begun my process of change, I had thought that most of my problems would correct themselves.

In time I learned to investigate those areas of my life which made me uncomfortable, and started to sort out what wasn't working.

As this was happening, things became clearer. I'm working through what's left, with God's hand and guidance.

May 3

Most of the coping mechanisms that I used to rely upon became liabilities, and are no longer desirable to me.

Understanding, being patient and waiting on God has allowed me to build some rewarding new habits.

Morals, virtues and spiritual principles are now my assets.

May 4

Even though I'm on a better path and rising to be obedient to God's will, at times, my own tolerance does wear thin.

When that happens, my growing slows down because I find myself stuck in pride and ego.

In those moments of clarity when I recognize what is happening, I let go.

May 5

"Through a 12 step program I've learned that the subject is me." ~ Dion

The importance of studying is to get a clear understanding on the subject.

I practice. I practice. I practice. I practice. I practice. I practice. I practice.

May 6

Part of living right is being able to do the right things for the right reasons.

However small or great, or the harm that I've done in the past to people, I have come to learn that I must make right my wrongs in order to grow.

May 7

I used to hide from the realities needed for healthy relationships. Things like being committed, being open-minded and being truthful were not my reality, when it came to people, places, and things.

I also didn't think apologies were needed.

Emotionally I was torn up from within. Now I have begun to see that God is teaching me to tell the truth.

May 8

I used to find myself feeling uneasy or guilty about circumstances in my life.

Now I see that the pressure comes from within me. I realize that I don't have to allow alienation to characterize who I would truly like to be.

May 9

Some of my behavior caused deep wounds to my soul. Even though I remember those times, I don't let them continue to hold me down or allow them to be excuses to keep me from moving forward.

Let's come to understand why we are here – to find and fulfill our purpose.

Through God I am building hope and finding comfort. I am grateful.

May 10

In the beginning, this journey started out as personal. Then the MIRACLE happened.

What I'm learning for myself can make a difference for others. I cannot keep progress to myself and so Making Individual Recovery A Community Lifestyle Everywhere is necessary.

As we continue doing our part, we become responsible, productive members in society.

May 11

We are always looking for the easier, softer ways out. When I begin to go back and think selfishly, God shows up. I am reminded of the importance and comfort of staying connected.

May 12

As I am becoming more spiritually connected with God, I realize that most of our struggles are because of lack of faith and obedience.

I'm not better than anybody else just because I chose to change the direction of my life through God's guidance.

I hope that those in my past and present are willing to embrace the positive changes. Even if they don't, I find comfort that these new choices are helping me.

May 13

What God is doing for me daily, man couldn't do in a lifetime. What matters is what I do with each day.

Today I am grateful for clarity, confidence and demonstration.

May 14

We are growing each day that we share and practice doing something of value with our new freedom.

We have developed a new, positive frame of reference, and this frame came when we began to trust others and what they where suggesting.

May 15

Time will pass and often we will think about when we started to change.

As we expand we must focus on the blessings that come from doing more of what we learned at the very start.

May 16

Everything I do in life has a beginning and ending. Although struggles will happen, my attitude about what happens doesn't have to hold me captive.

We come to learn to live in harmony with ourselves and others so that we can live in emotional freedom.

May 17

The more I learn to understand God; I become aware that I had been my worst enemy.

I allowed grief and sorrow to become fear that used to overwhelm me.

Today I don't run from my emotions for they are part of life on life's terms.

May 18

There is no need to be afraid of what we used to do or romance thoughts about how we used to act.

With inner strength, be courageous and face the fears.

May 19

How do we handle being back on that playground visiting that old familiar pain?

We don't! Some battles have already been fought. The same God who has been carrying us has also fought those battles.

May 20

Don't let ego trick you into thinking that doing service, praising God, or studying the Word is boring, slow or "not cool."

In humility and obedience is service and joy.

May 21

My relationship with God today has come through someone waiting at the crossroads. Waiting to point me down the path with courage, He always seems to be at the right place at the right time.

May 22

I had a feeling that certain people had my best interest at heart, and I trusted enough to get to know them.

I realize that none of what I've maintained or any of my successes have come without the help of others.

I thank God for the ability to learn and build friendships.

May 23

What I have come to learn is that at times, my Higher Power speaks through people, ones with whom we can build relationships.

Especially in times when we want pity or sympathy, they give us "tough love" as we are going through.

They become the links we need, telling us the truth and pointing us in the right direction.

May 24

Friends are there for us when we're not there for ourselves.

Sometimes they may not be aware of the impact that they have. We must embrace these same loving and caring attitudes and pass them on to others.

May 25

Before I didn't know much about being in relationships. However, kind words from people became the light that I needed to push me through with courage.

May 26

Your mind has room for only one thought at a time. At which point, it's that first thought that really speaks to you. When that happens, check in and ask...

Am I honestly in touch with my actions, my motives and myself? Or do I just give in to pride and ego and make bad decisions?

Through my prayer and meditation I receive strength to maintain my spiritual connection.

May 27

"Here's an interesting phenomenon about gratitude: I had none and I didn't care about anything. I had no feelings of guilt, shame or remorse. I was not grateful.

One day I stopped and prayed. What came out of that prayer was a surprise to me. I prayed for God's will for me and the power to carry it out. He gave it to me. I learned gratitude."
~ Dion

Today I give what was so freely given me to help others.

May 28

Daily maintenance of prayer and meditation keeps me on sound spiritual footing. By feeding my mind in this way and filling it with gratitude, there isn't room for negativity.

May 29

I am granted a daily reprieve each day I wake up. I have the chance to be of service. I can encourage and motivate. I am grateful for my life and I try to keep it simple by staying out of selfishness and keeping my priorities first.

I find joy and courage while standing on a solid foundation.

May 30

I establish and improve my conscious contact with God, by being positive and aware of the messages that I send and receive to and from each person with whom I interact.

In doing so I expect nothing in return and that is one more step closer to thriving in this new way of life.

May 31

The first thing we do is change the pattern of being self-destructive.

I stop taking shortcuts, lying, manipulating and practicing the other habits that have been so natural to my old way of life.

I learn to be disciplined and obedient – smashing my pride and ego. God is preparing me as I stand up under fire and endure the cleansing of my mind.

June 1

We can easily get set back in life's everyday problems when we stop the practicing of spiritual principles.

In moments of clarity, filled with hope, we have motivation and a driving force of comfort for ourselves.

That same hope that was so freely given to us pulls others and ourselves forward.

June 2

Our secrets cause us more harm than good when we keep them completely to ourselves.

We cannot receive God's blessings when we hold back and don't share important things with others.

When we open up, we no longer deny ourselves and those we care about the beauty of the moment.

June 3

Secrets can kill us. If we continue to allow our secrets to be in control, they drive a deeper wedge between our Higher Power, our newfound peace and us.

Freedom is the same way – we can't experience it without honesty and truthfulness.

June 4

No longer must we deny or regret our past; we keep the door cracked on yesterday so we can remember that pain. What happened didn't kill us.

I use these memories and spiritual principles to keep me motivated not to return.

June 5

I had been breaking promises for years; mostly to people whom I love.

Even though I have begun to change, sometimes throughout my day I get complacent and stuck on stupid.

In this moment, I recognize that it's never too late to keep my promises, admit my faults and show those in my life how much they matter.

June 6

We examine our lives, admit our wrongs, make amends and sincerely try to change our behavior; after all, it is hard trying to move forward if we are looking back.

June 7

Often as individuals we start out with good intentions at staying outside of self, and going the distance to put on a good front just enough to keep us in the race.

And while we're so busy keeping up, we ignore our souls, the inner voice, that is telling us that it really wants to learn, to encourage and to teach our neighborhood, community and nation to read, write and develop.

We need to take action everyday to keep our relationship with God, ourselves and other human beings alive.

I'd like to think that if His will is God's gift to me, then my actions are my gift to God.

June 8

In the beginning of my spiritual journey, I was on a roll and things started going well. I was grateful and knew that God actually cared about me.

I was encouraged and thought everything would be great from here on out because the little things were adding up. I was making progress and felt it.

I worked to get the material together, building a structure and maintaining it. Staying connected to God is necessary because even though I'm still encouraged, some days are not easy.

June 9

From the start of our journey we were filled with fear, loneliness, and guilt as we struggled to find new meaning in our lives.

We started seeking daily guidance from anyone and everyone out of desperation. We believed that once we got through our circumstance, once we achieved our goals, once we were able to solve our problems, then we would have some peace.

We apply efforts to our most obvious problems, working through them step by step and learning and letting go of the rest.

By staying open and accepting the (love) spiritual principles, and the (understanding) God's will for us, we continue to evolve and change.

June 10

Why do we often choose not to surrender unless we have some assurance there is something worth surrendering to?

Is it because most of us have been at the receiving end of an injustice that we thought had sabotaged our life?

Did we allow life to become a breeding ground for many of the resentments that we developed?

When I become acquainted with my inner self, God and spiritual practices, I begin to put them into action and I start to grow.

I begin to be grateful not only for having an understanding of spiritual principles, but for the quality of life I am receiving from a God I am learning to understand.

June 11

For years we have wandered in darkness without direction, relying only on instinct, suspecting everyone, trusting no one.

We need to check regularly to make sure we set boundaries, have clarity and stand accountable for our actions.

I do the job at hand, and as I progress, new opportunities for improvement present themselves. I now know that with God's blessing the teaching is never over, I'm never on my own and everyday is brand new.

June 12

There are no mandates, laws or commandments when it comes to freedom of choice. However, every time we judge the behavior of another, we cease to see them as potential friends and fellow travelers on the road. Our pain then grows and our freedom is limited.

What we're really putting off is the freedom we get from letting go of judgment.

June 13

Change is free, not forced.

Freedom allows me to recapture the dignity that was crushed by the burden of being preoccupied with holding on to things that are beyond my control.

June 14

If we don't tell someone that we are hurting, they will seldom see it.

I now understand that emotions that I had suppressed have begun to surface. The amount of darkness surrounding me only proved to me just how I had gotten so attached to the messed up stuff I did and how I became. I was living in my own illusion.

I didn't know how to identify my feelings nor did I pay attention to how that pain feels.

By asking for help and trying out the recommendations, I learn what my dreams are and pay attention to what I really want.

June 15

When we finally sit down and dig deep I bet we can see all kinds of dreams buried.

There is so much crap on top of those dreams you must shovel it off. Start by creating your list of justifiable actions, creative excuses, dubious luxuries, justifiable resentments, wrongs others have done to you, judgments, anger, self-pity, self-righteousness, false pride, false humility and humongous egos.

Reflect on when you first began to want to change and how you didn't want to accept God. Now, go ahead and take the risk, let these things out and let them go.

You have already been thinking about something you denied yourself a long time ago. Each action we take, each positive change we make builds our self-esteem. We realize that we are beginning to think differently. We are living ourselves into "right thinking."

June 16

As I continue walking this path to righteousness I'm learning the value of relationships that I have with others.

I'm thinking about God and want to do the right things for the right reasons. This is the direct result of building personal relationships with people who used to be sources of irritation to me.

I have found tolerance to be a principle that strengthens not only my foundation but also my relationships. However, I also continue building my relationship with God and I'm learning to understand.

June 17

When we are prepared, we must try our newfound way of life. Our experience reveals that working and living by spiritual principles is our best guarantee against the evil that men do.

We isolate time to pray and meditate, trying to figure out God's will. As we think about the defects and the experiences surrounding them, they reassure us that pride, ego and stubbornness don't work.

When I honestly become willing to be taught, I trust that God will continue to help me now and in the future.

June 18

Why is it such a big deal to always be right or to be in the middle of all the action?

Is it because we are so comfortable with being in the spotlight? Or maybe it's because our defects have been our constant companions, filling our comfortable imaginations?

Yes, it's fun to be on the ride and some may say that it's ok to keep up with the Jones'.

However, we cannot afford to lose sight of the importance of doing the right thing for the right reasons.

June 19

There's a difference between fighting with a problem and pushing through the resistance that the problem brings into our lives.

When we face dilemmas and struggle to do the right thing, we are still having difficulties, and that means we're fighting with the problem. It's usually our ego or pride that will destroy the day if given authority.

Each of the spiritual ideals that we are learning to understand serves to straighten out kinks in our thinking. We are accepting that we can only be governed by a loving God.

June 20

Our experience shows that if our principles become an extension of the personality, ego or attitude, we lose effectiveness.

Before I'm able to completely let go and move from allowing ego to control me, I will want to clear the air, admit that I have been wrong and ask my Higher Power to remove whatever defects may prevent me from being helpful and constructive.

June 21

Freedom is not automatic when we turn away from defects or when we decide to stop our old behavior.

We pray, seeking knowledge greater than our own. We open our minds and keep them open. We become teachable and take advantage of what others have to share with us.

We then find the courage to end that downward momentum we have been struggling with to have serenity and to experience freedom.

June 22

Fear is something else.

Our fears can keep us from connecting with the world around. Our fears can also shield us from those who might be trying to influence our thoughts to do wrong when we are at our weakest state.

The pressure we let build up from fear sometimes comes from within us. At other times it's external, based on the situation or based on what dilemma that presents itself.

It's for this reason that we must keep our focus personal and work on an honest program that will allow us to generate courage from the fear and rise above influences that mean us harm.

June 23

Our attitudes are problems that can become obsessions. If we are harboring attitudes about money, property, prestige or a relationship, they find ways to become pebbles on our path. When this happens, it shuts us off from our spiritual aim.

Each one of us, no matter what our personal make up, has a unique way of identifying our problems when we adjust our attitudes and are receptive.

There are people around us who are willing to connect with us – be it friends, family or a caring stranger who offers a smile or kind word.

Chances are that at some time in our day when our behavior is off balance we come across someone who will reach us when no one else can.

June 24

Instead of fussing and worrying about how different you are, be grateful that you're unique.

We all have to pull together and understand that we are part of something greater than ourselves.

Being self-centered and withholding from others makes you unavailable. This can stop you, and even those who need you, from growing, maturing or flourishing.

Seek knowledge in prayer and meditation on how to greet the circumstances that come in your own unique way.

June 25

Through the activity of study, mediation, prayer and faith, I receive the power I need to maintain my freedom each day.

I've reached an exciting stage in my life now that I am coming to some understanding of God. I must continue to look for ways to show my gratitude. I see more and more for which to be grateful.

June 26

When we allow our emotions to be in control, they become destructive. We overlook the everyday things that really matter when we begin to sit on the pity-pot of selfishness.

We stay connected through gratitude, obedience and discipline, not allowing our ego to go unchecked.

June 27

Often we find ourselves interacting with people from all walks of life, many with different backgrounds.

Too many days are devoted to feeding into our ego and resentments, influencing us to act out and trying to control.

One of the most important things we can do to further our primary purpose is to be willing to accept that we are actors as part of the play, not the director of the stage.

June 28

The drive for prideful gain in the areas of attitude, emotion and behavior that brought so much pain in the past falls by the wayside, if we adhere to principles.

Ultimately we can become willing to take care of ourselves and nurture ourselves through whatever experience ego may bring.

June 29

After I came out of darkness and stopped relying on self, it took a while before I began to understand why I must seek wisdom and knowledge.

We find ourselves depending on human beings in risky situations, trying to satisfy an obsession or a compulsion. They fall short of perfection and so do we.

There is nothing that we can cling to in this world that's long term. Although relationships, secure employment and living in that ideal house feels good, we can't do it on our own.

No person or thing can restore our sanity, care for us, or be unconditionally available and loving whenever we are in need.

June 30

Often we've heard it said, "Don't hate the player hate the game," just to come to the finish and find ourselves let down.

We are accustomed to placing all of our eggs in one basket until we overcome our fear. However, to get what you want takes time, work, patience and effort.

Holding on to resentment keeps us being in "hater mode." Eventually all that we hold dear will require us to let go, in some shape or form.

Don't get angry when the time comes in your life to let go, open your heart to that person, place, or thing, and to say thanks for teaching you to LOVE and helping you to GROW.

July 1

Enslaved by our overwhelming need to be in control, our lives lack purpose and connection.

We find ourselves in situations where our ideals conflict. Being selfish and possessive conflicts with being committed and patient.

We gain power when we assume responsibility for our lifestyle. Then we have power to exert a positive influence on our decision-making, loved ones and the spiritual principles by which we live.

Therefore, surrender is not failure; rather it is a smashing of our ego that wants to dictate our purpose.

July 2

I get so excited about this new attitude and the things happening in my life that sometimes I put aside my responsibilities and purpose to change.

This double standard of emotions holds us captive while in active addiction, and fills us with terror and confusion.

It's easy to romanticize what we don't know and become complacent in our progress, for this newness can be overwhelming. Rushing may have us tempted to put off important things until tomorrow.

We have to know that living by spiritual principles must be an everyday occurrence as well, not just something we ignore until tomorrow.

July 3

We can't sue, whine, or complain because we accepted the dangers of pride and ego.

We sign away our life fighting for the wrong cause, selling the wrong product, or when we are teaching dishonesty.

When we stop fighting with selfishness we move freely to serenity, security and comfort. No longer are we asking "Why?" to keep control. We ask "How?" and surrender our inability to manage our own life, giving ourselves the opportunity to become teachable and responsible in this society.

July 4

When we get a reprieve from life's ups and downs, some might say that we're standing at the turning point. We can move forward and continue growing and learning to stay out of self or we could stay stuck – being caught up on attitude, emotion and behavior.

The choice is yours.

We've been given support in courageously setting forth on a new path. We have also been given the gift of conscious contact with a Power greater than ourselves providing us with the inner strength and direction we so sorely lacked in the past.

July 5

There's magic in what we believe.

Our beliefs tell our future better than any crystal ball or psychic. At any time we are subject to delusion, denial, rationalization, justification or insanity, which are all hallmarks of typical selfish ways of thinking.

Knowing the depths of our character defects, we can still reach out with a loving and compassionate hand and know that our faith in God is developing.

July 6

Pain is a shortcoming that should be called a long going, because it often takes time for it to fade from our lives.

It's not good to want something or someone so much that the desire itself rules our lives. When unforeseen dilemmas rip at those things, it can cause feelings of torture if we allow fear, anger and resentment.

We open our hearts and become clear about what we want in our small and big choices. We are not perfect and making mistakes in our lives helps us to get clear to understand that pain has its place – in the past.

I start today with good intentions about what I want in terms of family, health, and a modicum of success in my career and in my relationships.

July 7

Now that we've begun to soul search, we have a certain awareness and intuition about what to do and what not to do. In the light of life, we come to know what is fake and what is real, and once in a while, that unexpected problem may very well be a blessing in disguise.

The only obstacle that blocks this flow of understanding is a closed mind. We get so caught up on reservations like "coulda, shoulda, woulda" that we become prisoners of our own thoughts and are condemned by our actions as we are trying to get back to the flow of life.

I choose not to miss out on the lessons that God is trying to get me to understand.

July 8

I must remember that my opinion comes from my experience and my reality comes from my perception.

How often do we see beyond what is in arm's reach as we walk along this chosen path, picking up lessons that God has laid?

I choose to be cautious as I step out, letting my path be full of awareness and gratitude. It's gratitude that reminds me that all things are possible with the help of God.

I surrender to circumstances in my life and I have courage to change the things I can. I live and let live.

July 9

Freedom from self-will and the conflict it generates in our lives breaks our reliance on ego.

We fill that gap between our intention and behavior, seeing positive results manifest in reality.

July 10

When our ideas, desires and demands take first place in our lives, we do things differently because our priorities have changed.

I must experience the inner change though it may be painful, because it guides me from self-ishness to self-lessness if I'm to have freedom.

July 11

No longer do we exclude ourselves from the flow of life.

We started by making our intention to live a meaningful life clear to ourselves. We now remove the excess so that we continue to grow stronger and healthier.

July 12

Studying to gain understanding may not be entertaining but it is real, true and life saving. It allows me to gain knowledge and I start to dream again.

My new vision brings joyful feelings of what's coming next from the God whom I am coming to understand.

July 13

When I take an honest inventory of myself daily I get an inkling of where I see myself.

I see me doing good things today and in the future. It's funny how God gets my attention.

July 14

Honesty is an important tool that allows me to see beyond appearances and first impressions. As I continue to develop the habit of being honest, it becomes a gift that allows me to visualize.

Visualization creates matter out of spiritual energy through meditation.

July 15

Our lives are progressing nicely. Things are going well and each day brings more spiritual and even material gifts. We no longer have to run in fear from the defects and liabilities that used to plague our lives.

July 16

The fear of facing my problems and myself kept me at a standstill.

A lot of things in life will seem like too much to bear if we try to see them all as one big thing. I break situations down and keep it simple.

July 17

One thing I've learned is that when starting new endeavors we are truly humble. I think because the sense of the unknown keeps us cautionary and patient.

It's when we think we know and get relaxed that we get cocky in our efforts.

July 18

I will always have the prerogative and the responsibility to bring down my ego and pride to their most manageable level. This happens because I continue to pray and meditate every day.

July 19

No matter how unreasonable others may seem, or how much I tend to make excuses, I do not give up. No longer do I scare myself out of doing the easiest things in life like going to church, praying and being responsible.

I am learning to forgive.

July 20

Are you saying "No!" to something in your life to which you'd like to say "Yes!"?

I no longer have to carry burdens of the past. I am eager to set goals and experience the fulfilling relationships that life has for me.

July 21

Sometimes I would talk myself out of blessings. At times I also felt unworthy to receive them.

I am learning to talk myself into accepting them now.

Forgiveness must come from within. As I forgive, I am able to reach out and touch others from my heart.

July 22

The power we find in spiritual principles is the power we lack on our own.

July 23

Even though I learn to simplify things, I know that my pace may be different than others.

I become patient with my progress.

July 24

The keys of my success are teaching me that it is not a particular event that is of prime importance.

But it is my spiritual condition that gives me light and hope as I move forward.

July 25

To maintain my freedom I must give daily attention to working on my inner feelings.

I've been taught not to react to outward circumstances.

July 26

When my spiritual condition is positive I react positively.

If I already knew how to do everything, I wouldn't need the experiences in my life to teach me the lessons!

July 27

We've put in the time and energy towards visualizing positive events.

We have learned not to react in our old way. No longer do I dwell in circumstances.

July 28

I take a moment to reflect on the emotional upheaval my will, words and life choices may cause.

Just because we have the creative powers to imagine doesn't mean we have total control over our actions.

July 29

It was our ideas and attitudes about the world that made it impossible for us to find a comfortable place in it.

Being teachable, humble and accepting allows us to play our part and see the best for ourselves as we move through.

July 30

To insure our vision of life is in focus, we have to bring our ideas in line with reality, prayer and meditation.

Taking inventory is the key to sound thinking and positive action for me.

July 31

We learn that if we pray and meditate regularly, we won't be hurting as often or as intensely.

A basic premise of mediation is that it is difficult, if not impossible, to obtain conscious contact unless our mind is still.

August 1

Sometimes the unexpected things that manifest are better than what we can imagine or see.

We rise above any limiting thoughts as meditation brings more moments of clarity through spirituality.

August 2

Meditation allows me to develop spiritually in my own way. It can be difficult because of my propensity toward ego, fear and pride.

As I continue to practice it gets easier.

August 3

My willingness to admit when I am at fault facilitates the progression of my growth.

Meditating and studying regularly helps me to maintain my growth, courage and willingness.

August 4

Through prayer we seek conscious contact with our God.

Through unremitting inventories of myself, I admit, acknowledge and accept responsibility for any wrong-doing.

August 5

If you find yourself using your imaginative power to create negative events: STOP!

We grasp limitless strength through our daily prayer and surrender, as long as we keep faith and renew it.

August 6

As I reflect on yesterday's struggles, I realize that I lacked serenity based on my beliefs and experiences.

Today I focus on God's will, not my problems, and trust that He will manage my day.

August 7

Worries of yesterday and the fear of tomorrow's deadlines denied me the calm I needed to be effective each day.

In this moment I pray that God will show me His will, and that He will help me carry that out.

August 8

Defects like gossip and manipulation sneak into my life when I am not making a constant effort in my studying.

My daily results measure how much meditation and prayer is working. I live through guidance and clarity.

August 9

Sometimes we get so focused on what we don't want and what we're afraid of that our vision becomes jaded. The negativity becomes all we can see.

When we remove our selfish motives and pray for guidance, we find feelings of peace and serenity.

August 10

We do the footwork and accept what's been given to us freely on a daily basis.

We remind ourselves that our uniqueness is the blessing of us being willing and humble to do God's will.

August 11

Receiving the full meaning and power of the Word is a continual process. It does not mean occasionally, or frequently. It means throughout each day.

We encourage each other to seek strength and guidance according to our belief in Him.

August 12

Sometimes we search for joy and enlightenment so frantically that we don't see the brilliance at our own feet.

Without studying spiritual principles it is unlikely that we could experience a spiritual awakening. So lighten up!

August 13

Don't let your hopes and expectations be so high that you miss the beauty in what joy is.

We now know that if we ask for a daily reprieve, it will be granted.

August 14

Many times what we need isn't a change of scenery, but a renewed vision of what is already there.

We begin to realize that as long as our spiritual needs are met, our problems are reduced to a point of comfort.

August 15

The spiritual principles of honesty, open-mindedness, and willingness can help us correct our problems and prevent their recurrence.

In order to rebuild our character, we'll find it necessary to maintain those values.

August 16

A lot of our chief concerns and major difficulties come from our experience in with living without morals.

If we ignore our values, we'll discover that the biggest fibs we've told have been the ones we've told ourselves.

August 17

We went from self-destructive patterns of life to a new influence in our personality. The spiritual foundation we are building brings about this experience through fellowship with God.

August 18

We don't use people or drugs anymore because the foundation we are building does not allow the mixture of oil and water, good and bad. We learn early in our construction that the wrong material – the wrong measurements – would cause flaws in our foundation.

August 19

Our deepest secrets only have power over us when we keep them hidden.

On our journey we have to be careful of what we share and with whom we share our thoughts. Releasing the shame, guilt or remorse that may come with those secrets is important. Until we share them we will not be free of those defects that keep us sick.

August 20

I keep my thoughts focused on God throughout my days because my mind wanders off and I find myself stuck when I don't.

This direct contact with my Higher Power is to keep my thoughts pure. I am able to make clear decisions that help me to maintain positive changes.

August 21

At one period of time I used to beat up on myself, and I was pointing the finger at all the wrong people. When I started working on a spiritual plan, I began to change my outlook towards me. I was not as hard on myself and I gave myself a break.

By taking a chance, I stepped out on faith with some people who didn't look like the people I was used to seeing.

August 22

I went through some relationships with people that were not necessarily good or bad. Stepping on toes of my friends does not work.

I've learned through growing up and developing a conscious, to do the right things in life.

August 23

The secret of fulfilling my potential is acknowledging my limitations and believing that time is a gift, not a threat.

Hope is the key that unlocks the door of discouragement.

August 24

Many years of my life revolved solely around selfishness. Contemplating failure had always smashed my hope.

Today I have been given a gift that has allowed me to experience success. Faith is allowing me to make it through.

August 25

The essence of all growth is willingness to seek how to remove our shortcomings.

We develop a working appreciation through a spiritual program. We gain humility and courage by disclosing ourselves to our Higher Power.

August 26

How many times did we allow impatience to cause us to have rude awakenings? Impatience is one of the many barriers that block us from spiritual progress.

We remove those barriers one day at a time knowing that this is a life-long process!

August 27

In the past, we didn't know what love was and that concern and caring only got us so far.

Submission to God was the first step to changing that. Now comes other definite and practical steps we can take to show love for ourselves, whether we feel that love or not.

August 28

How many times have we allowed small things to become big challenges in our lives? How many times have we failed at something and allowed emotional pain to become a distraction?

We surrender to the will of God after the storms to find peace within.

August 29

Osmosis has nothing to do with working a spiritual program. Invariably, we find that at some point we made a decision to clean up our life and to do the right things.

We have to start from the inside first and the outside will become clean. This freedom only comes from doing God's will.

August 30

Are you focusing on the circumstance or do you need something tangible to help you understand what the lesson is?

Instead of asking "Why?" ask: "What is the lesson?"

For we may not be aware of how destructive resentments actually are.

August 31

Have you noticed that when faced with chaos and confusion we seem to lose all knowledge and the dis-ease seems to be your best friend?

Through fellowship and relationship with God we find peace to sit in the midst of the storm.

September 1

Through daily work with spiritual principles we get needed perspectives and insights on how we can work toward solutions.

We continue to learn new and previously undiscovered things about ourselves.

September 2

We had been so used to "playing God" that we've believed most of the results. The spiritual principles teach us that we have no real control when life's wild fires are raging through our lives.

We keep our hearts open and stay aware, for the disease is always haunting.

September 3

We no longer have to live our lives in isolation because we're not trying to control what we can't.

We discard that prideful ego and replace it with a steady strength that comes from a power greater than ourselves.

September 4

Our behavior was dictated by the weeds of our addiction and this left an empty space in our lives, filled with dark and cold feelings.

We place in this space a loving and caring God whom we are coming to understand.

September 5

Through an odd series of coincidences and fear we are paralyzed and stop growing. We created an empty space that we don't have to be afraid of.

Courage is not the absence of fear. Willingness to walk through it is!

September 6

Prayer was something we had to get used to and to practice on a daily basis.

When keeping close contact with our Higher Power we become more serene. What really matters is what's in our heart.

September 7

We come to understand ourselves and appropriate ways to handle the wreckage from our past.

We have to understand it, name it, learn from it and release it, in order to grow through it.

September 8

When we begin the healing process, it takes much more than abstinence from things that aren't working.

Manifest what you need from a place of responsibility, trust and peace. Then experience the gifts of life.

September 9

Today I don't have to struggle or exert my will.

I use the resources and gifts that have been given and apply some simple spiritual principles in my life daily. I then gain more freedom.

September 10

As I continue this journey, I diligently walk these miles at my own pace, being cautious of my actions and how I respond to situations.

For I have learned that I don't have to face decisions alone.

September 11

Happiness doesn't depend on my outward circumstances.

I no longer react to the criticism of others. My new life is rich and full of willingness that comes from within.

September 12

We must trust the principles that we are taught, for feelings and resentments can sabotage our love.

The freedom we get from learning brings back dignity that was crushed by selfishness.

September 13

Now that I'm much more comfortable with me, I must pass on things that will help others.

As we come to know truth, we understand that it's our responsibility to carry a clear message of hope to sensitive ears the same way we would want to receive it.

September 14

There is limitless strength available to us whenever we need it.

We've already accepted and admitted our part. Now all we have to do is be obedient as we continue to seek knowledge to gain understanding from God, who is loving and caring.

September 15

Life is too big for me to tackle by my own power.

When I take appropriate action through practicing my spiritual program, I learn that dreams can come true.

September 16

No one owes you anything and the sooner you accept this, then you can start and continue to forgive yourself and others.

September 17

It's better not to expect people to take care of me because if I become lazy, I turn into the problem instead of the solution.

We each have good qualities we can share with others. Through shared experiences we gain independence and freedom. We know that our dependence is on God.

September 18

You are a vital, vibrant soul that came here to experience, grow and change.

You and what you are becoming are valuable to those around you. Remember that love grows only when it is shared.

September 19

Procrastination is limiting. It creates hopelessness and voids, which lead us into taking each moment for granted.

It tricks me into thinking that where I have been, and where I am now, are all that are available to me.

The spiritual principles show me the importance of service and sharing, which helps to fill any void and shows me limitless opportunities and possibilities.

September 20

Obedience teaches me a new and greater understanding. I realize that I lack power on my own. Being obedient helps show me who I am and where to find that Power.

September 21

I let go of any irrational thoughts, which is a process of ego deflation. I let myself be creative and listen to my inner voice, the one that guides me through humility into courage.

This allows me to grow as an individual.

September 22

Patience is an understanding of our emotions that allow us to respond, not react, to our feelings when they are in conflict with the common good.

September 23

Encouraging my inner power to surge allows me to set aside personal ambition, fear and anger.

Emotional balance can mean finding and maintaining a positive outlook on life.

September 24

Being still doesn't necessarily mean we are inoperative. For me, it simply means that I can see the forest through the trees when I let go and let God.

September 25

I recognize and believe in the good within myself. I do what I need to do to become efficient and operate with ease.

September 26

Sometimes we need a change of scenery.

If we want to live differently, then we have to move beyond fear of growth and selfishness.

September 27

Experience teaches us about slowing down, being still and letting things be the way they are.

Principle teaches us not to do the same things and expect different results.

September 28

If we sacrifice our honesty and integrity to avoid conflicts or disagreements, we are robbing ourselves of the vitality and joy available in our lives right now.

September 29

We can keep ourselves so busy living up to an image that we put the lesson on the back burner.

However, we must continue to study in order to apply spiritual principles. When we get clarity, we gain freedom and also learn the lesson.

September 30

Being complacent, even as we grow, keeps us confined to limited experiences.

"Fame" gained by trying to maintain a certain image or to fit in fades all too quickly when we don't have a solid foundation.

Status doesn't matter if we don't share it with others.

October 1

We often multiply our joys and divide our burdens by sharing them.

This allows us to have serenity and peace of mind.

October 2

The spiritual principles and the power to practice them give me the direction and courage I need to change.

I am enjoying freedom.

October 3

Many of us resist doing things differently. It takes courage to step out into the unknown.

When willingness emerges, a glimmer of light begins to touch my soul.

October 4

Letting Go and Letting God means that we apply spiritual principles to each and every area of our lives.

When we do that, we accept the defects that have existed and allow Him to turn our experiences and personal traits into assets.

October 5

As we are growing, our relationships are strengthening, because we know that we are not flourishing on our own.

We are influenced and impacted by those who touch and guide us to meet our responsibilities in life.

I am able to reach out and help others.

October 6

Our prayers will be shaped by our experience with spiritual principles. Now my Higher Power is making me a channel of His Word, thoughts and deeds.

October 7

We need to remember that our actions will impact those around us. I must be willing to do His work so that He can function through me successfully.

October 8

My personal understanding of my Higher Power allows me to take responsibility for how I touch and connect with everything and everyone in my life today.

October 9

Let your personality, in all its glories, foibles and eccentricities, come shining through, as you remain connected in understanding to your Higher Power. Your problems vanish as you reach out of a once trembling soul.

October 10

While our lifestyle doesn't come with an extended warranty, there is a routine maintenance schedule that's necessary. It is to refine us and enhance our experiences.

October 11

The purpose of spiritual growth is not to eliminate the personality; it is to expand it on a higher plane. When this happens we no longer neglect the gifts we've been given.

October 12

When I forget to seek a higher state of consciousness I'm also robbing myself of the love, friendship, unparalleled experiences, possibilities, moments of clarity, and peace of mind which come with life on life's new terms.

October 13

What a wonderful awakening for me it is to realize that of myself I'm nothing, yet when I put God first, it keeps me sane.

October 14

If I fail to step up to my responsibilities and acknowledge them on a daily basis, it only limits my ability to receive God's love and grace.

October 15

Everyday isn't peaches and cream. Don't get caught up thinking and feeling that every day and will be sweet.

October 16

God only requires me to maintain my spiritual connection. I don't get caught up in trying to become perfect because that is impossible. I live one day at a time to stay centered and comfortable in our relationship.

October 17

No longer must we endanger, humiliate or abuse ourselves or others just to get the next fix.

Our freedom is based in relief, truth and brotherly love.

October 18

Sometimes we have to look to see what our gifts will be. Surrender, courage and hope are what make our program unique.

October 19

The pleasure that comes with being free can be as simple as a hug, harmonious relationships with loved ones, and being productive members of society.

We are blessed with guidance and care from God, whom we are learning to understand.

October 20

Joy comes from ongoing and active study as well as application of the principles. We need to know in our hearts and souls that we're okay whether we ever get whatever we're after or not.

October 21

I am learning that wholeness relates directly to the process of detaching and letting go. I need only to bring into my understanding willingness to grow, and allow God to have His way with me.

October 22

Joy is not the absence of pain, it is the gift of continued spiritual awakening. We learn to refrain from doing things we might want to hide.

October 23

Low self-esteem and how it manifests itself had become a way to cope with painful events.

Today I am using ways that lead to action, honesty and openness as the Higher Power is healing throughout my life.

October 24

Note to Self:

Do not cope with painful events by devaluing yourself.

Are you willing to believe in and pursue the reason and purpose for your life?

October 25

Ignorance is killing us. Respond to life by loving and taking care of you. Gradually, the destructive force of selfishness is being replaced by the life giving force of God.

October 26

When facing dilemmas are you telling yourself that you are complete without the guidance and strength of a Higher Power?

"Check in. I'm just sayin.'" ~ *Dion*

October 27

Ignoring the disorder won't make it disappear. We all want and need daily necessities. It would be impossible to proceed through the various stages of reconstruction without them.

October 28

Help yourself to a healthy dose of completeness and letting go. We gain a deep sense of satisfaction from making our amends. Proof comes when we see the results of God's work on our behalf.

October 29

God grants me the power I need for maintaining spiritual growth.

October 30

We touched a lot of people casually when living in our lost days. Some we want to make direct amends to. Through courtesy and kindness we are able to give back the way God would have us to give.

October 31

Some of us substitute self-esteem for what we wear, how much money we make, and what we possess.

My spiritual armor provided by God, gives me confidence and emotional balance. I am at peace with myself.

November 1

Many of us come from backgrounds where betrayal and insensitivity among friends were common occurrences. We then convinced ourselves that we could make it alone and we then proceeded to live life on that basis.

Practicing nonresistance when people wanted to argue and learning to say "Hmmm," instead of engaging in battle, kept my life and environment calm.

Once I admitted powerlessness, I learned to connect with my Power. I also learned to push against the wind. I understood that those who didn't keep practicing spiritual principles on a daily basis faced a rough road.

November 2

We thought we were hopelessly bad, or even insane, for accepting constant beat downs to our self-esteem.

Today I love myself because I know I am somebody.

November 3

Flies always seem to hang out around the waste.

Are you the one spewing it? Before you open your mouth to speak, or make a decision to act, be careful about the way you respond. Can you smell it?

November 4

I spent many years letting fear of abandonment control me. This fear affected my relationships with family and friends, and my environment in everyday living.

I am learning to remove the defects and fears that threaten my freedom, peace and moments of clarity.

November 5

As we mature on our spiritual journey we get the same kind of benefits from spending as we do from paying our monthly obligations.

Taking responsibility points the way to a more serene place by letting me clear away my past.

November 6

We are each walking our own path regardless of fears, desires or actions, justified or not.

Even though life is not fair, I'm responsible for my side of the street.

November 7

Our initial response to any type of instruction or direction was often negative. As we become spiritually receptive, this allows us to connect in our relationships as well. We realize we do have a place.

Being a part of the cast, I can make the entire production stronger.

November 8

Sometimes we want to rebel, especially when we feel justified. When that feeling comes from instinct, it can get us into trouble. By tuning to intuition, we can choose which battles to fight.

Not everyone is the CEO or leading man. Be part of the solution and you can be a working star.

November 9

We find that what others did to us was not as important as how we responded to the situation.

I enjoy serenity, but only when I entrust my life totally to God.

November 10

If left to themselves our resentments can lead us away from our new found freedom.

I've stopped fighting and surrendered entirely to my Higher Power.

November 11

Old habits die hard. Success rarely happens overnight or in seven days.

Somewhere between the good we do and the defects we have, is truth.

November 12

There's no quick fix, or panacea that will work for every person.

The studying of spiritual principles enables me to close the door on my former lifestyle and be open to new avenues.

November 13

The spiritual principles have allowed you to see and set goals for yourself.

However, don't be taken by false claims of overnight success and instant enlightenment along your path.

November 14

Although I have some experience now of doing God's will, true change takes time and effort especially when I'm changing and tackling big issues.

November 15

When the glow of peace and freedom begins to fade, I examine what's been tried and true. That means I must rise up to my new circumstances and what my life now requires.

I can relate to the experience and the life lessons, and use this knowledge as a basis for understanding.

November 16

Sometimes life deals wounds that can't be eased by even the most heartfelt words.

It is the very humbling of self that has me hold to my Higher Power. I allow Him to bring comfort and healing.

November 17

When nothing in our lives feels right, sometimes the answer isn't in doing or searching frantically.

My responsibility is to sit still, try to be patient, and to be in the moment as God clarifies the next move.

November 18

Honesty is the only hope I have if I am to continue healing.

For the miracle comes when we accept, believe and trust that who we are right now is who we need to be.

November 19

My life felt like an ongoing series of errors and when the winds of life blew, I found that I was broken.

Yet, with the help of OGs and wisdom from God, I was able to reach within. I found strength and surrendered.

November 20

My ego had turned life itself into a constant cycle of isolation, humiliation and dereliction.

Being aware of my true nature is the best way to gain freedom from the controlling, manipulative behaviors imposed by self and ego.

November 21

The beautiful irony of the spiritual principles is that in our own surrender we find flexibility, learn to silence the chattering of our ego, and walk with a sense of freedom.

November 22

During my dis-ease I broke many rules. The very thing I feared the most was not knowing what's in store.

I no longer allow fear to impede on my freedom to change.

November 23

I make a daily effort to cause no further harm to me or to others. It is so important for me to stay out of the way, otherwise I will hurt Us.

This helps me to keep me in check.

November 24

We make the decision to finally step outside of self. However, some days we forget about our commitment. Through spiritual principles, we learn to stay committed and to be accountable for our actions.

November 25

How do we say, "Take my will and my life and show me how to live," only to become selfish?

We have to mean what we say and say what we mean.

November 26

As we progress along our own journey, our thinking is still unhealthy at times.

Yet, we begin to recognize that we are not the only ones. We hear some of the most ridiculous nonsense and realize that self-centeredness blocks so many blessings.

November 27

We find hope and understanding when we open up and people can relate to what we have to share.

If all we do is listen then we remain congested with our private thoughts, fears and hurt feelings.

Applying spiritual principles in our relationships and conversations creates balance, wisdom, and allows us solutions when we face dilemmas.

November 28

With great expectations and care, our loved ones often motivate our progress. When we share stories and create new experiences together, it gives us a special comfort like no other.

We appreciate their acceptance, honesty, actions and feelings, especially when they are vocalized.

November 29

At times enslavement still threatens my desires and even my dreams. Sure, I've accomplished so many goals. Yet, I cannot become complacent.

I continually move forward along my own journey, denying the power of outward defects to trick me into feeling satisfied and content.

November 30

What is it worth to face your past fears? It's priceless!

We've moved through so much to get to this point. We stand grateful that we said, "No!" when it counted.

I am encouraged and motivated by the progress thus far and I allow my radiating inner force to see me through.

December 1

Today I have options that I did not have in the past. I am able to see what's real and what's important.

By being willing, I make decisions and choices to do the work and not expect instant gratification.

December 2

Despite the challenges that come with day-to-day living, my journey is much smoother.

I continue to put in the necessary energy in order to maintain a solid foundation.

December 3

When we momentarily screen things, mental blocks can force us into a false sense of self-pity.

When we rely on approval or opinions from others, it is usually based in low self-esteem thinking.

I take time to stop and consider a more broad view.

December 4

We can mediate our choices when we realize that the approval of others will not fill our voids.

Satisfaction can be found in realizing that through making some mistakes we both learn and receive valuable lessons.

December 5

Most of my days were spent living in darkness. I was confused, full of emotions and my actions were negative and limited.

There was no visible end to the madness of which I had isolated myself. I had every reason to be skeptical since I didn't have hope.

No longer is my past a locked autobiography. My life serves as a reference to be openly shared.

December 6

The spiritual principles are where the light, and not theories, shine. This happens when I admit and become willing.

I consciously remember that willingness gets me through shame and allows me to be patient. Guidance manifests itself through my inner wisdom.

I do not allow shame to stop me from enlarging my spiritual relationship with myself. I am courageous as I allow understanding to be the beacon that gets me through hard times.

December 7

When caught up in being selfish I forget that it causes pain. I know that chemicals are an addict's elixir. Am I addicted to material things?

Painful obsession binds me to unhealthy thoughts of worldly gain. I can't afford the price of selfishness, as it costs so much more than my peace.

December 8

I don't get caught up in the false reality of instant gratification and the misperception that I can take a few days off from practicing my spiritual principles.

I know that romancing unhealthy thoughts is like opening the window to dis-ease. I find myself banging on the door for help.

My daily reprieve continues to enlarge my spirituality.

December 9

I allowed feelings to keep me running in fear. The perception that I couldn't do certain things damaged my esteem.

Now remorse becomes a tool to help me achieve power over those things that would deceive me. I continue to clean up my house and willingly accept change.

December 10

It's time to review our motives behind our plans. If they are not pure in heart and God-centered, then our plans will fail.

We prevail when we develop a giant in our spirit by living in moral principles.

December 11

Have you been selling the wrong products? It doesn't make you a bad person; it just means you need new inventory.

We realize that we are not bad people; we've made bad decisions.

Bad feelings happen when we haven't accepted the consequences of our actions. We understand that our Higher Power's grace gives us the courage to accept the good.

December 12

The secret of fulfilling my potential is acknowledging and overcoming my limitations.

Patience is believing that time is a gift and not a threat.

Hope is the key that unlocks the door of discouragement, and willingness comes from me knowing the difference.

December 13

Often my actions revolved around my selfishness. Contemplation and failure had smashed my desires.

Today is a gift that allows me to make it through mistakes and to understand the lessons that I have overlooked.

December 14

I remember that the essence of growth is willingness. I remove shortcomings as I continue to develop a working appreciation through a design for living.

We gain humility and courage by disclosing ourselves to our Higher Power.

December 15

Why do we rationalize and sit on that pity-pot, acting like it is comfortable?

We remove the bonds of fear, anger and doubt. We stay active and know that faith is at work.

December 16

What used to stand in the way of my being useful to God were the small annoyances and the grief that kept me distracted.

Life is too dear today to pay the price of living in darkness.

December 17

We gave up our pride and self-will to a Power greater than ourselves and life seems balanced.

Sometimes it seems so good that we start to put our spiritual principles second. Remember that the same application process that got us here is the very same process that we must continue to apply. We remain grateful.

December 18

Placing ourselves in risky situations was something common for us, and this compromised our freedom.

Lying is just one of the many defects that keeps us in bondage. By staying honest we know the truth and this keeps us free.

December 19

We have come to a place in our lives where we need to step up and take bigger steps in faith.

For we have learned how to be honest, open- minded and willing. This continuing processing is a crucial part of our foundation built on God.

December 20

We have to stop waiting for "the rescue team" to bring us life support.

Courage is the guiding force in all our affairs because we understand where it comes from. This is a walk show not a talk show.

December 21

We have survived so many catastrophes.

I am thankful for the mercy and grace that God has given me to live and breathe today.

I am grateful for the courage to stand up, walk right and do the things that used to scare me.

December 22

I relax in the comfort of knowing that I am walking in God's will.

I allow humility and trust to guide me into peace, productivity and to greater accomplishments in life and in my spiritual journey.

December 23

As I continue to pray, mediate and listen, my relationship with God remains my lifeline.

I receive my instructions through faith in the daily practicing of spiritual principles. This supports my foundation.

December 24

Honesty allows me to face unruly emotions and process seemingly unmanageable situations.

I feel good about who I see in the mirror and I welcome healthy interactions and relationships. Being connected is a joyful experience.

December 25

Now that I am aware that my life has purpose, I celebrate my existence.

I lighten up and I enthusiastically give all of myself, good and bad, to do the will of God.

December 26

Trusting the spiritual process, I know that at times I will struggle when facing certain obstacles and people from my past.

I call on my Higher Power to provide the fortitude and guidance needed to remain calm, make it through the storm and make good choices.

December 27

Peace through prayer and meditation provides the conscious contact with God that I need to get me through every single day.

As I listen and am obedient, the answers and clarity settle into my spirit and soothe my soul.

December 28

Guidance from God has turned my worst faults into my greatest assets.

When I seek to restore balance, my heart and soul continue to heal and I am available for whatever comes next.

December 29

The road to success takes time, hard work and tenacity to move forward. I also realize that it is not a destination, it is a journey.

With my spiritual foundation I allow my God to be the force that pushes me to new heights and pulls me through when elements try and keep me back. I remain grounded in His Word.

December 30

Our road to joy is no longer a pipe dream.

Daily, we look at ourselves and the positive things we've said, done and experienced as blessings and gifts.

I am grateful for the people and circumstances that surround me, as I share my destiny.

December 31

I love God. I must study and stay on the path of my spiritual journey and continue to live in my life's purpose.

I admit and acknowledge that the essence behind my existence is the service I am to provide in helping others.

Heartbreak, anger and madness lead me to find comfort. Through reading I build hope.

I rejoice in knowing that and I am trustworthy and deserving enough to love and be loved in return. Because my life matters, I share my activities and myself with my Higher Power.

I stand grateful for the strength, power, connection and moments of clarity.

A NOTE FROM THE PUBLISHER

Mission Possible Press...

Creating Legacies through Absolute Good Works

As a publisher I have the opportunity to transform hopeful writers into successful authors. This brings me great pleasure because I believe everyone has wisdom to share and valuable stories to tell.

Prior to publication, I worked with Dion to help him crystallize his mediations and was thoroughly blessed by the experience. *A man who has been through many challenges, bad decisions, tough choices; who openly admits to having been selfish and stubborn; then willingly surrenders to a better life through his relationship with God; and then share it with others, is not only a rare find, he's a treasure.*

Personally, I am grateful to him for sharing his journey with me and allowing me to use my experience as a leadership trainer & coach to walk him through what he wanted to share with you. The content and process were renewing and refreshing; and the mediations also filled my own soul and spirit.

Professionally, Dion as an author also validated the reason that Mission Possible Press exists – to meet people where they are and to help them rise to who they are meant to be. We are all about *Extraordinary Living and Sharing it with Others.* So, hats off and hearts open to new perspectives, new thoughts, new feelings and new choices to restore the lives of individuals and of people around the world because everyone matters.

Thanks to Dion Thorpe, we are *Building Hope and Finding Comfort DAILY!* I am honored and pleased to present this book as part of our Extraordinary Living Series.

In the Spirit of Communication,

Jo Lena Johnson,
Founder and Publisher

Mission Possible Press, a division of Absolute Good
AbsoluteGoodBooks.com

About the Author

Author Dion Thorpe and his wife Yolanda are partners in love and in life. Together they own and operate *Hands on Detailing*, a full service car detailing operation located in midtown St. Louis City, their hometown.

A man who knows the value of community and the importance of service, Dion enjoys fishing, reading, writing and mentoring. He owns dogs, is a part of the Masonic family, and volunteers as a Little League assistant football coach. Annually he provides Christmas toys and clothing to hundreds of children ages 6 to 11 who would not normally have them. Dion is the proud father of Sierra, Tiara, Dionica, Marquees, Dion, Brandon and Riley.

Finally, Dion strongly supports the young people who come to work for him by teaching them skills, work ethic and the importance of responsible citizenship.